Comptroller of the Currency
Administrator of National Banks

I0448784

Home Mortgage Disclosure

Comptroller's Handbook

February 2010

CCE

Consumer Compliance Examination

Home Mortgage Disclosure

Table of Contents

This booklet provides background information and optional expanded examination procedures for the Home Mortgage Disclosure Act and Regulation C. Examiners will select which of these procedures are necessary, if any, after first completing the core assessment as outlined in the "Large Bank Supervision" and "Community Bank Supervision" booklets of the *Comptroller's Handbook.*

These procedures document technical compliance with Regulation C. Also, the HMDA data play a critical role in both the Office of the Comptroller of the Currency's (OCC) fair lending and Community Reinvestment Act (CRA) examination processes. Examiners review these data in light of fair lending risk as described in the Fair Lending Examination Procedures Booklet of the *Comptroller's Handbook,* and to support lending performance in CRA examinations as outlined in the Community Reinvestment Act Examination Procedures Booklet of the *Comptroller's Handbook.*

Background and Summary

The Home Mortgage Disclosure Act (HMDA) was enacted by the Congress in 1975 and is implemented by the Federal Reserve Board's Regulation C (12 CFR 203). The period of 1988 through 1992 saw substantial changes to HMDA. Especially significant were the amendments to the act in the Financial Institutions Reform, Recovery, and Enforcement Act of 1989 (FIRREA). Coverage was expanded in the FIRREA amendments to include many independent nondepository mortgage lenders, in addition to the previously covered banks, savings associations, and credit unions. Coverage of independent mortgage bankers was further expanded effective January 1, 1993, with the implementation of amendments in the Federal Deposit Insurance Corporation Improvement Act of 1991 (FDICIA). For a more detailed discussion of the history of HMDA, see the FFIEC's Web site at www.ffiec.gov/hmda/history2.htm.

HMDA grew out of public concern over credit shortages in certain urban neighborhoods. The Congress believed that some financial institutions had contributed to the decline of some geographic areas by failing to provide adequate home financing to qualified applicants on reasonable terms and conditions. Thus, one purpose of HMDA and Regulation C is to provide the public with information that will help show whether financial institutions are serving the housing credit needs of their neighborhoods and communities. A second purpose is to aid public officials in targeting public investments from the private sector to areas where they are needed. Finally, the FIRREA amendments of 1989 require the collection and disclosure of data about applicant and borrower characteristics to assist in identifying possible discriminatory lending patterns and enforcing antidiscrimination statutes.

As the name implies, HMDA is a disclosure law that relies upon public scrutiny for its effectiveness. It does not prohibit any specific activity of lenders, and it does not establish a quota system of mortgage loans to be made in any metropolitan statistical area (MSA) or other geographic area as defined by the Office of Management and Budget.

Financial institutions must report data regarding loan originations, applications, and loan purchases, as well as requests under a preapproval program (as defined in section 203.2(b)) if the preapproval request is denied or results in the origination of a home purchase loan. HMDA requires lenders to report the ethnicity, race, gender, and gross income of mortgage applicants and borrowers. Lenders must also report information regarding the pricing of the loan and whether the loan is subject to the Home Ownership and Equity Protection Act, 15 USC 1639. Additionally, lenders must identify the type of purchaser for mortgage loans that they sell. Some lenders have the option of indicating the reasons for their decisions to deny a loan application. Lenders regulated by the OCC, OTS, and NCUA must indicate the reasons for denial.

Regulation C requires financial institutions to report lending data to their supervisory agencies on a loan-by-loan and application-by-application basis by way of a "register" reporting format. The supervisory agencies, through the Federal Financial Institutions Examination Council (FFIEC), compile this information in the form of individual disclosure statements for each institution, and in the form of aggregate reports for all covered institutions within each MSA or metropolitan division (MD).[1] In addition, the FFIEC produces other aggregate reports that show lending patterns by median age of homes and by the central city or noncentral city location of the property. The public may obtain the individual disclosures and aggregate reports from the

---

[1] A metropolitan division is a subset of an MSA having a single core with a population of 2.5 million or more.

FFIEC Web site (www.ffiec.gov/HMDA) or from central depositories located in each MSA or MD. Individual disclosure statements may also be obtained from financial institutions.

The supervisory agencies use the HMDA data as a screening tool to identify aspects of a financial institution's mortgage activities that may warrant scrutiny to determine whether discriminatory practices are present. The data do not include important determinants of loan pricing and qualifications, however, and thus, one cannot draw definitive conclusions about whether particular financial institutions discriminate unlawfully based solely on the HMDA data.

Applicability

The regulation covers two categories of financial institutions — "banks, savings associations, and credit unions" and "mortgage lending institutions." The regulation applies to a bank, savings association, or a credit union that meets the following criteria:

- On the preceding December 31, had assets exceeding a specified annually published amount (as of December 31, 2009, that amount was $39 million);
- On the preceding December 31, had a home or branch office in an MSA;
- In the preceding calendar year, originated at least one first lien home-purchase loan (or a refinancing of such loan) on a one- to four-family dwelling; and
- Meets one of the following criteria: (1) it is federally insured or regulated; (2) the mortgage loan referred to above was federally guaranteed, insured, or supplemented; or (3) the institution intended to sell the mortgage loan to Fannie Mae or Freddie Mac.

A for-profit nondepository "mortgage lending institution" is covered if it meets all of the following descriptions:

- In the preceding calendar year, it originated home purchase loans (including refinancings of home purchase loans) that either (1) equaled 10 percent or more of its loan origination volume, measured in dollars or (2) equaled $25 million or more;

- On the preceding December 31, it had a home or branch office in an MSA;[2] and
- Either (1) on the preceding December 31, it had total assets of more than $10 million, counting the assets of any parent corporation, or (2) in the preceding calendar year, it originated at least 100 home purchase loans or refinancings of home purchase loans.

The definition of a mortgage lending institution applies to a mortgage lending subsidiary in which a depository institution owns a majority interest and, since 1990, to independent mortgage companies. HMDA has covered the mortgage lending subsidiaries of bank holding companies, savings and loan holding companies, and savings and loan service corporations since 1988. Mortgage lending subsidiaries are treated as distinct from their "parent," and must file separate reports with their parent's supervisory agency.

For purposes of this discussion and this booklet's examination procedures, the term "financial institution" will apply to both a depository and a nondepository institution.

Compilation of Loan Data

For each calendar year, a financial institution must report data regarding its applications, originations, and purchases of home purchase loans, home improvement loans, and refinancings. Loans secured by real estate that are neither refinancings nor made for home purchase or home improvement are not reported. Data must also be given for loan applications that did not result in originations, including applications denied, withdrawn, or closed for incompleteness, as well as applications approved by the institution but not accepted by the applicant. Required reporting also includes certain denials of requests for preapproval of a home purchase loan under a program in which a lender issues a written commitment to lend to a creditworthy borrower up to a specific amount for a specific time.

---

[2] The institution may or may not have a physical presence in the MSA per section 203.2(c)(2) of Regulation C, which states that a nondepository mortgage lending institution is deemed to have a branch office in an MSA if, in the preceding calendar year, it received applications for, originated, or purchased five or more purchase or home-improvement loans on property located in that MSA.

Loan Purpose

For each application or loan, institutions are required to identify the purpose (home purchase, home improvement, or refinancing), lien status, and occupancy status of the property relating to the loan or loan application (owner-occupied as a principal dwelling). As defined by Regulation C, a home purchase loan is one secured by a dwelling and made for the purpose of purchasing that (or another) dwelling. A dwelling is a residential structure that may or may not be attached to real property, located in a state, the District of Columbia, or the Commonwealth of Puerto Rico. It includes an individual condominium or cooperative unit, a mobile or manufactured home, and a multifamily structure, such as an apartment building.

A home improvement loan is defined as one that is at least, in part, for the purpose of repairing, rehabilitating, remodeling, or improving a dwelling or the real property on which the dwelling stands. Home improvement loans not secured by a dwelling should be reported only if the institution classifies the loan as a home improvement loan. Dwelling-secured home improvement loans should be reported without regard to classification.

Finally, a refinancing is defined as a transaction in which a new obligation satisfies and replaces an existing obligation by the same borrower. For coverage purposes (*i.e.,* to determine whether or not an institution is covered by the HMDA), the existing obligation must be a home purchase loan and both the new and existing obligation must be secured by first liens on dwellings. For reporting purposes, both the existing obligation and the new obligations must be secured by liens on dwellings.

Loan Type

The regulation requires financial institutions to identify the following general loan types: conventional, FHA-insured, VA-guaranteed, and FSA/RHS (Farm Service Agency/Rural Housing Service) guaranteed.

General Loan Information

The amount of the loan or the loan application, application date, action date, and the type of action taken must be reported.

Property Type

Institutions must report the property type as a one- to four-family dwelling, multifamily dwelling, or manufactured housing.

Property Location

Financial institutions must report certain geographic data for loans on, and applications for, properties in any MSA where the institution has a home or branch office. These geographic data are optional for loans on properties located outside these MSAs or outside any MSA, unless the financial institution is subject to additional data-reporting requirements under the Community Reinvestment Act (CRA). The reported geographic data consists of the MSA or MD number,[3] state and county codes, and the census tract[4] number of the property to which the loan or loan application relates.

Institutions subject to both CRA and HMDA data-reporting requirements must collect and report geographic data for all loans and applications (whether located in an MSA or not), not just for loans and applications relating to property in MSAs where the institution has a home or branch office.

Applicant Information

Institutions must report the following data for applications and on originated loans: the applicant's or borrower's ethnicity, race, sex, and gross annual income. Reporting these data on purchased loans is optional. Lenders must ask applicants and borrowers for information regarding their ethnicity, race, and the sex even if applications are made entirely by telephone, mail, or the Internet. If an applicant submitting his or her application in person fails to provide the information, the lender must note the information from the applicant's appearance or surname, filling in the appropriate blanks on the application for the applicant. Regulation C contains a model form that can be used for the collection of data on ethnicity, race, and sex. Alternatively, lenders can use the form designed to obtain information under 12 CFR

---

[3] In the case of an MSA divided into metropolitan divisions (MDs), the relevant unit for this purpose is the MD.

[4] In a county with less than 30,000 in population, the institution may enter NA, or the census tract number, at the institution's option.

202.13 of the Federal Reserve Board's Regulation B (Equal Credit Opportunity).

Purchased Loans

If an institution originates or purchases a loan and then sells it in the same calendar year, it must report the type of entity that purchased the loan. Except in the case of large secondary market purchasers such as Fannie Mae and Freddie Mac, the exact purchaser need not be identified. For example, an institution may indicate that it had sold a loan to a bank, without identifying the particular bank.

Pricing-Related Data

Institutions must report the rate spread between the annual percentage rate (APR) and the average prime offer rate for a comparable transaction as of the date the interest rate is set if the spread is equal to or greater than 1.5 percentage points for first-lien loans, or equal to or greater than 3.5 percentage points for subordinate-lien loans.[5] The rate-spread reporting is required only on originations of home purchase loans, dwelling-secured home improvement loans, and refinancings. To determine the applicable rate spread, the financial institution may use the table published on the FFIEC's Web site (www.ffiec.gov/hmda) entitled "Average Prime Offer Rates Tables."

The following are excluded from the rate-spread reporting requirement: (1) applications that are incomplete, withdrawn, denied, or approved but not accepted; (2) purchased loans; (3) home-improvement loans not secured by a dwelling; (4) assumptions; (5) home equity lines of credit; and (6) loans not subject to Regulation Z.

Lenders must also report whether the loan is subject to the Home Ownership and Equity Protection Act (HOEPA), 15 USC 1639. A loan becomes subject to

---

[5] Lenders will use the new rate spread reporting test on loans for which applications are taken on and after October 1, 2009, and for all loans consummated on or after January 1, 2010, (regardless of their application dates). For loans for which applications were taken before October 1, 2009, and that were consummated in 2009, the revised rules do not apply. Lenders will apply the existing rate-spread reporting test, using Treasury security yield benchmarks, for those loans. For loans for which applications were taken before October 1, 2009, and that are consummated in 2010 or later, the revised rules apply.

HOEPA when the APR or the points and fees on the loan exceed the HOEPA triggers. Additional information on HOEPA coverage is found in the Truth in Lending booklet of the *Comptroller's Handbook*.

Lien Status

Lenders must report the lien status of the loan or application — first lien, subordinate lien, or not secured by a lien on a dwelling.

Denial Reasons and Other Data

Financial institutions regulated by the OCC, the OTS, and the NCUA, including subsidiaries of national banks and savings associations, are required to provide reasons for denials. Providing reasons for denials is optional for financial institutions supervised by the Federal Reserve and the FDIC. Institutions may also choose to report certain requests for preapproval that are approved by the institution but not accepted by the applicant and home equity lines of credit made in whole or in part for the purpose of home improvement or home purchase.

Excluded Data

A financial institution should not report loan data for:

- Loans originated or purchased by the institution acting as trustee or in some other fiduciary capacity;

- Loans on unimproved land;

- Temporary financing (such as bridge or construction loans);

- The purchase of an interest in a pool of loans (such as mortgage-participation certificates);

- The purchase of mortgage loan servicing rights; or

- Loans originated prior to the current reporting year and acquired as part of a merger or acquisition or acquisition of all the assets and liabilities of a branch office as purchased loans.

Reporting Format

Financial institutions record data regarding each application for, and each origination and purchase of, home purchase loans, home improvement loans, and refinancings on a loan/application register, also known as the HMDA-LAR. Financial institutions also record data regarding requests under a preapproval program (as defined in section 203.2(b)), but only if the preapproval request is denied or leads to the origination of a home purchase loan. Transactions are to be reported for the year in which final action was taken. As an example, financial institutions report a loan application pending at the end of the calendar year on the HMDA-LAR for the following year, when the final disposition is made. Loans originated or purchased during the calendar year must be reported for the calendar year of origination even if they were subsequently sold.

The HMDA-LAR is accompanied by a list of codes to be used for each entry on the form. See Appendix A to Regulation C for detailed instructions and guidance on the requirements for the register. For additional information review the FFIEC publication, "A Guide to HMDA Reporting: Getting it Right!," available on the FFIEC Web site.

Financial institutions must record data about a loan or application on the HMDA-LAR within 30 calendar days of the end of the calendar quarter in which the institution takes its final action. Entries need not be grouped in any prescribed fashion. For example, an institution could record home purchase loans and home improvement loans together on one register or separately on two registers. Each branch location may keep a separate register or the financial institution may keep a single register at a centralized location for the entire institution. In either case, however, a consolidated register for the entire financial institution must be submitted to the relevant supervisory agency.

For each calendar year, a financial institution must submit its HMDA-LAR, accompanied by a transmittal sheet, to its supervisory agency. Unless it has 25 or fewer reportable transactions, an institution must submit its data in automated form. For registers submitted in paper form, two copies must be mailed to the institution's supervisory agency. Institutions can submit their HMDA-LAR by e-mail to hmdasub@frb.gov. For both automated and hard-copy submissions, the layout of the register used must conform exactly to that of the register published by the Federal Reserve Board as Appendix A to Regulation C.

OCC regulated national banks and their mortgage subsidiaries that report more than 25 HMDA-LAR entries, must submit their HMDA-LAR for each year in an automated, machine readable form to the FFIEC by March 1 of the following year. Those national banks and mortgage subsidiaries that report 25 or fewer HMDA-LAR entries may submit their data in paper form. Using that data, the FFIEC produces a disclosure statement for each institution, cross-tabulating the individual loan data in various groupings, as well as an aggregate report for each MSA. The FFIEC posts these disclosure statements at www.ffiec.gov/hmda. Disclosure statements are no longer mailed to individual financial institutions.

Disclosure

As the result of amendments to the HMDA incorporated within the Housing and Community Development Act of 1992, an institution must make its disclosure statement available to the public at its home office within three business days after it is posted to the FFIEC Web site. It must also place the disclosure statement, for each of the prior two calendar years, in its CRA public file. An institution must also either (1) make its disclosure statement available to the public in at least one branch office in each additional MSA or MD where it has offices within 10 business days of the statement's posting on the FFIEC Web site or (2) post the address for requests in each branch office in each additional MSA or MD where it has offices. Institutions must send the disclosure statement no more than 15 calendar days after receiving a written request.

Also, an institution must make its loan application register available to the public after deleting the following fields: application or loan number, date application received, and date of action taken. These deletions are required to protect the privacy of applicants and borrowers. The modified HMDA-LAR for a given year must be publicly available by March 31 of the following year for requests received on or before March 1, and within 30 calendar days for requests received after March 1.

A financial institution must retain its full (unmodified) HMDA-LAR for at least three years for examination purposes. It must also be prepared to make each modified HMDA-LAR available for three years and each FFIEC disclosure statement available for five years. Institutions may impose reasonable fees for costs incurred in providing or producing the data for public release.

Institutions must post a notice at their home office and at each branch in an MSA, to notify the public that the disclosure statements are available. The Regulation C Commentary at 203.5(e)-1 contains a suggested notice that institutions can use.

The FFIEC also produces aggregate tables to illustrate the lending activity of all covered financial institutions in each MSA or MD. These tables and the individual disclosure statements are available on the FFIEC Web site, www.ffiec.gov/hmda, and through central depositories, such as libraries, in each MSA or MD. A list of the depositories is also available on the FFIEC Web site.

Administrative Enforcement

Compliance with the act and regulation is enforced by the OCC for national banks and their operating subsidiaries and federal branches and federal agencies of foreign banks. Administrative sanctions, including civil money penalties, may be imposed by the OCC for noncompliance.

An error in compiling or recording loan data is not a violation of the act or the regulation if it was unintentional and occurred despite the maintenance of adequate procedures for preventing such errors.

Accuracy in Preparing HMDA-LAR

The modified HMDA-LAR and the FFIEC-issued disclosure statement are principal sources of information for mortgage lending analyses conducted by the OCC, media, bank customer groups, and others. Analyses are often included in comment letters on bank merger and other applications. Institutions must maintain appropriate procedures to ensure that HMDA-LAR data are accurate.

An institution's procedures and verification systems could include internal testing to verify HMDA-LAR data with loan applications and property location sources (MSA, census tract, state, and county codes). Data for inclusion in the annual HMDA-LAR submission should be verified for accuracy and submitted according to Federal Reserve Board reporting instructions. Institutions should ensure that their reporting systems capture all HMDA-reportable transactions from all lending areas within the institution (e.g., mortgage department, installment loan department, private banking, and commercial lending).

Home Mortgage Disclosure   Examination Objectives

1. To assess the quality of the bank's compliance risk management system to ensure compliance with the HMDA and Regulation C.

2. To determine the reliability of the bank's compliance risk management system, including internal controls, policies, procedures, and compliance review and audit functions for the HMDA and Regulation C.

3. To determine the accuracy and timeliness of the financial institution's submitted HMDA-LAR.

4. To initiate corrective action when policies or internal controls are deficient, or when violations of law or regulation are identified.

Home Mortgage Disclosure   Examination Procedures

Examiners should assess the strength of the bank's risk management process and determine the bank's level of compliance with the Home Mortgage Disclosure Act (HMDA) and Regulation C. Use these procedures to review, test or validate bank internal controls, procedures and processes in those areas where the bank's risk management system does not adequately mitigate consumer compliance risk as documented in the core assessment, which is described in the "Large Bank Supervision" and "Community Bank Supervision" booklets of the *Comptroller's Handbook*.

Objective: To determine the adequacy and reliability of the bank's compliance risk process to ensure compliance with the HMDA and Regulation C and to ensure that its reported data are accurate and filed in a timely manner. The worksheet in Appendix A can be used to document the adequacy of the bank's HMDA and Regulation C compliance process.

1. Review appropriate bank records and workpapers to document the bank's and any covered subsidiaries' process (es) and internal controls for collecting, verifying, and reporting HMDA data using the HMDA worksheet, and determine whether the internal controls ensure that data are reliable by determining whether:

   - Bank verification procedures include samples that cover all home purchase, home improvement, and refinancing loan types.

   - Sample sizes meet the minimum guidelines in the OCC's "Sampling Methodologies" booklet of the *Comptroller's Handbook*.

   - The work performed is accurate by reviewing the supporting documentation for the testing that was conducted.

   - Steps are taken to correct identified deficiencies.

   - Significant deficiencies and their causes are included in reports to management/board.

   - Corrective actions are timely and appropriate.

- The area is reviewed at an appropriate time interval.

If you determine that the bank's process and internal controls are adequate and that the data are reliable but the OCC has **not** previously tested the accuracy of the bank's reported HMDA data, proceed to the next objective. If, since the last OCC test, changes were made in systems or controls that affect data gathering or data quality, or the bank's internal testing indicates that controls are not being effectively maintained, perform the relevant steps in the next objective. If the process and internal controls are adequate and the OCC has previously tested reportable data at the bank at least once and determined the data to be reliable, perform step #7 in the next objective and complete the examination activity.

Regardless of the adequacy of the bank's process or internal controls, if the OCC or the bank has found the data to be unreliable (a significant level of errors), proceed to the next objective.

Objective: To determine the accuracy of the HMDA data and whether the data can be used in helping to evaluate the bank's CRA performance. The worksheet in Appendix B can be used to document the accuracy of the bank's reported HMDA data. (This objective can be completed as a stand-alone activity or in conjunction with fair lending examinations or CRA evaluations.)

Note: These procedures should be adjusted to reflect work that may already have been performed during other supervisory activities or during periodic updates that are part of the CRA examination strategy phase. (See the Large Bank CRA Examiner Guidance, OCC Bulletin 2000-35.)

1. Determine whether HMDA data will be verified and the evaluation period to be reviewed. (If in conjunction with a large bank CRA examination, perform this step at least 30 days prior to the start of the data verification phase of the CRA examination cycle.) If HMDA data is to be verified, prepare and submit the data verification request letter to the bank. A sample data verification request letter is in Appendix III of the Large Bank CRA Examiner Guidance. The examiner should customize the letter for the bank that is being reviewed and should ensure that data requests cover only items needed to complete the review. The request letter should be discussed with bank managers to ensure that they understand what has been requested and when it is needed.

2. Determine whether HMDA data are accurately collected, maintained, and reported by selecting and testing a sample of HMDA loan application records. Use the guidance for **numerical sampling** in the "Sampling Methodologies" booklet of the *Comptroller's Handbook* to select the sample. Use the highest possible reliability and precision when selecting samples.

   When reviewing HMDA data, key fields are loan type, loan purpose, property type, owner occupancy, loan amount, action taken type, MSA/MD, state, county, census tract, applicant ethnicity, co-applicant ethnicity, applicant race, co-applicant race, applicant sex, co-applicant sex, income, type of purchaser, request for preapproval, lien status, rate spread, and HOEPA status.

   Errors in HMDA data are considered **significant** when:

   - At least 5 percent of the loan application records contain errors in key fields; or

   - It is the examiner's judgment that the bank's level of errors prevents an accurate evaluation of the bank's HMDA lending performance.

   If you determine that the bank's data are reliable, and the OCC can use the data to conduct analyses and form conclusions, proceed to step 7. If not, proceed to step 3.

3. If you determine that the level of errors in the bank's reportable HMDA loans is significant,

   - Discuss the errors with bank management and determine the cause of the errors by identifying weaknesses in internal controls, compliance review/audit, training, management oversight, or other factors.

   - Inform the bank that it must correct the data. If applicable, determine from discussions with management whether the timing of the CRA data analysis phase of the CRA examination will be affected. Allow the bank a reasonable amount of time to make the corrections.

- If verification of the HMDA data is in conjunction with a large bank CRA examination or a fair lending examination, with input from the supervisory office, determine whether to postpone the CRA or fair lending examination to allow the bank time to correct the data, considering:

  - The extent and history of data problem(s),
  - The type of data that are unreliable,
  - The relevance of the flawed data to the accurate CRA rating of the bank,
  - Examiner resource constraints,
  - Pending corporate applications, and
  - Any other relevant considerations.

- Document the weaknesses in the bank's processes and/or internal controls that led to the inaccurate data. If the inaccurate data are indicative of systemic internal control weaknesses at the bank, bring this to the attention of the bank EIC.

- Determine whether the bank will be asked to resubmit its HMDA data once they are corrected, after consulting the supervisory office. Consider the following resubmission guidelines if the timing of resubmission will allow corrected data to become part of national aggregate data. (The OCC will not require a bank to resubmit specific year data if the FFIEC has already published the aggregate tables for that year. However, in all cases the HMDA data must be corrected and retained in the bank.)

  HMDA data resubmission should be considered if any of the following descriptions applies:

  - Any one key field is incorrectly reported for at least 5 percent of the loan application records sampled;

  - At least 10 percent of the bank's loan application records sampled have an error in at least one of the key fields; or

  - Errors in submitted data prevent an accurate evaluation of the bank's CRA performance.

- Determine whether HMDA errors warrant consideration of civil money penalties (CMPs). CMPs should be considered when an institution has submitted erroneous HMDA data and has not established adequate procedures to ensure the accuracy of the data. Complete a CMP matrix for HMDA violations on any bank that meets any of the following guidelines:

  - The bank has been required to resubmit data based on findings at consecutive examinations;

  - Resubmitted data are still erroneous and have an error rate that exceeds the resubmission guidelines;

  - The bank has greater than a 5 percent error rate in four or more key fields for loan application records sampled; or

  - The bank has errors in at least one of the key fields for more than 40 percent of the loan application records sampled.

- Inform bank management of your findings and communicate what needs to be done to correct the data.

- Adjust the CRA strategy and time line to reflect follow-up activities, as appropriate.

- After the bank responds that the necessary corrections have been made, review any changes to the bank's process for ensuring accurate data and test the corrected data (the extent of the testing depends on the extent of the problem):

  - Numerically sample loan records in at least one problem area (i.e., geographic area, MSA/MD, loan type, or specific data error type) to test the bank's corrected data.

  - Use a minimum sample size of 60 loans for each problem area tested. (Refer to the "Sampling Methodologies" booklet of the *Comptroller's Handbook* for instructions.)

- Document results of the test, determining the adequacy of the bank's data integrity process.

- If the corrected data are reliable, retain data in electronic format for the CRA examination data analysis phase. If the data remain unreliable, proceed to step 4.

- Determine whether corrected data must be placed in the public file after consultation with the bank EIC. If required, inform the bank.

4. If the bank is unwilling or unable to correct errors in HMDA-reportable data, eliminate the loan product with inaccurate data from the data that are considered in the evaluation of the bank's CRA performance. In the event that the unreliable data are isolated to a specific geographic area, eliminate only that area's unreliable data, if feasible, from the data that are considered in the evaluation of the bank's CRA performance.

5. Consider whether the lack of reliable data may negatively affect large bank CRA component ratings, including lending, multistate MSA/MD or state ratings, and the management and compliance component ratings of the CAMELS/ITCC ratings. Do **not** assign a bank with unreliable data a composite CRA rating of "outstanding."

6. In coordination with the bank EIC and appropriate supervisory office, meet regularly with bank representatives to notify them of OCC activities and findings.

7. Document the data verification findings and conclusions. Briefly discuss how the accuracy of data was verified and conclusions drawn from that process. Note whether material errors were identified in the reported data and how the errors impaired your ability to evaluate the bank's CRA performance, if applicable. If you determined that the bank's data were unreliable, discuss the data problems in the PE and ROE, including the cause and regulatory response, and cite violations of HMDA in the ROE.

HMDA Worksheet

This worksheet can be used for reviewing audit workpapers and evaluating compliance risk management processes, including a review of bank policies and procedures and internal controls, as appropriate. Only complete those aspects of the worksheet that specifically relate to the issue(s) being reviewed, evaluated, or tested, and retain those completed sections in the workpapers.

When reviewing audit or evaluating compliance risk management processes, a "No" answer indicates a possible exception/deficiency and should be explained in the workpapers. When performing transaction testing, a "No" answer indicates a possible violation and should be explained in the workpapers. If a line item is not applicable within the area you are reviewing, just indicate "NA."

Underline the applicable use: Audit   Bank Policies   Training

HMDA Worksheet	Yes/No	Comments
Policies and Procedures Evaluation		
1. Policies and procedures are adequate, on an ongoing basis, to ensure compliance with the HMDA and Regulation C.		
2. The financial institution has assigned one or more individuals responsibility for oversight, data update, data entry, timely reporting of the data, and informing the board of directors of the results of all analyses in a timely manner.		
3. The financial institution maintains documentation for those loans it packages and sells to other institutions.		
4. The institution has established and implemented adequate controls to ensure the separation of duties (e.g., data entry, review, oversight, and approval).		
5. Internal reports or records document policies and procedures revisions and any informal self-assessments of the institution's compliance with the regulation.		
6. If the institution offers preapprovals, and if the institution's preapproval program meets the specifications detailed in Regulation C, its policies and procedures provide adequate guidance for the reporting of preapproval requests that are approved or denied in accordance with the regulation.		
7. The institution's policies and procedures address the reporting of (1) loans that are not secured by a dwelling and that are originated in whole or in part for home improvement and classified as such by the institution, and (2) dwelling-secured loans that are originated in whole or in part for home improvement, whether or not classified as such.		
8. The institution has established a method for determining and reporting the lien status for all		

HMDA Worksheet	Yes/No	Comments
originated loans and applications.		
9. The institution's policies and procedures contain guidance for collecting ethnicity, race, and sex data for all loan applications, including applications made by telephone, mail and the Internet.		
10. The institution's policies and procedures address the collection of the rate spread (difference between the APR and the average prime offer rate for a comparable transaction as of the date the interest rate is set), and the institution has established a system for tracking rate lock dates and calculating the rate spread.		
11. The institution's policies and procedures address how to determine whether a loan is subject to the Home Ownership and Equity Protection Act and the reporting of applications involving manufactured home loans.		
12. The HMDA-LAR is updated within 30 days after the end of each calendar quarter.		
13. The board of directors has established an independent review process of the policies, procedures, and HMDA data to ensure compliance and accuracy, and is advised each year of the accuracy and timeliness of the financial institution's data submissions.		
14. The institution has procedures to comply with the requirement to submit data in machine-readable form and to ensure the accuracy of the data that are submitted in machine-readable form.		
15. The institution's loan officers, including loan officers in the commercial loan department who may handle loan applications for HMDA-reportable loans, maintain appropriate documentation of the information entered on the HMDA-LAR.		
16. The financial institution has policies and procedures to ensure its modified HMDA-LAR is available to the public during the three-year term.		
17. The financial institution has policies and procedures to ensure its disclosure statement is available to the public during the five-year term.		
18. The financial institution has internal control processes to ensure that the persons who capture and code the data are doing so accurately and consistently.		
Audit Compliance Review Evaluation		
1. Internal review procedures and audit schedules comprehensively cover all of the pertinent regulatory requirements associated with HMDA and Regulation C.		
2. The audits or internal analyses performed include a reasonable amount of transactional analysis and written reports that detail findings and recommendations for corrective actions.		
3. Internal reviews include any regulatory changes that have occurred since the prior examination.		
4. The institution ensures effective corrective action (to correct past errors and prevent future ones) in response to previously identified deficiencies.		
5. The financial institution performs HMDA-LAR volume		

HMDA Worksheet	Yes/No	Comments
analysis from year to year to detect increases or decreases in activity for possible omissions of data.		
HMDA Training Evaluation		
1. The institution ensures that individuals assigned compliance responsibilities receive adequate training to ensure compliance with the requirements of the regulation.		
2. The individuals assigned responsibility for HMDA compliance:		
a. Possess an adequate level of knowledge and have established a method for staying abreast of changes to laws and regulations.		
b. Know whom to contact, at the financial institution or their supervisory agency, if they have questions not answered by the written materials.		
3. The individuals assigned responsibility for data-entry receive appropriate training in the completion of the HMDA-LAR and receive copies of Regulation C instructions for completion of the HMDA-LAR (Appendix A), the staff commentary to Regulation C, and the FFIEC's "Guide to HMDA Reporting: Getting it Right!" in a timely manner.		
4. The financial institution's loan officers, including loan officers in the commercial loan department who may handle loan applications reportable under the HMDA (including loans and applications for multi-family or mixed-use properties and small business refinances secured by residential real estate), are:		
a. Informed of the reporting requirements necessary to assemble the information.		
b. Familiar with the disclosure, reporting, and retention requirements associated with the loan application registers and the FFIEC public disclosure statements.		
c. Aware that civil money penalties may be imposed when an institution has submitted erroneous data and has not established adequate procedures to ensure the accuracy of the data.		
d. Aware that correction and resubmission of erroneous data may be required when data are incorrectly reported for any one key field in at least 5 percent of the loan application records.		
e. Familiar with the disclosure statements that are produced from the data.		
5. When data are collected at more than one branch location, the appropriate personnel are sufficiently trained to ensure that all branches are reporting data under the same guidelines.		
Compilation of Loan Data		
1. The financial institution collects the data in accordance with section 203.4(a) and Appendix A of the regulation.		
2. The HMDA-LAR is updated within 30 calendar days after the end of the quarter in which final action is taken. (203.4(a)		

HMDA Worksheet	Yes/No	Comments
3. The financial institution requests ethnicity, race, and sex data for all telephone, mail, and Internet applications in accordance with Appendix B of the regulation. (203.4(b)(1))		
4. For applications taken face-to-face, the financial institution obtains data concerning ethnicity, race, and sex by inference from the applicant's appearance or surname if the applicant chooses not to provide this information. (203.4(b)(1))		
Disclosure and Reporting		
1. The loan or applicant data are presented in the format prescribed in appendix A of the regulation. (203.4(a))		
2. The financial institution reports all applications for, originations of and purchases of home-purchase loans, home-improvement loans, and refinancings. (203.4(a))		
3. The financial institution did not report (203.4(d)):		
a. Loans originated or purchased by the financial institution acting in a fiduciary capacity (such as trustee).		
b. Loans on unimproved land.		
c. Temporary financing (such as a bridge or construction loan).		
d. Purchase of an interest in a pool of loans (such as mortgage-participation certificates, mortgage-backed securities, or real estate mortgage investment conduits).		
e. Purchase solely of the right to service loans.		
f. Loans originated prior to the current reporting year and acquired as part of a merger or acquisition or as part of the acquisition of all assets and liabilities of a branch office.		
g. A refinancing if, under the loan agreement, the financial institution is unconditionally obligated to refinance the obligation, or is obligated to refinance the obligation subject to conditions under the borrower's control. (Appendix I.A.5a)		
4. The financial institution submits its completed HMDA-LAR in automated machine-readable format by March 1 following the calendar year for which the data are compiled. (203.5(a)) *Note: Financial institutions that report 25 or fewer entries on their HMDA-LAR may collect and report their HMDA data in a paper form. Any financial institution opting to submit its data in such a manner must send two copies that are typed or computer printed. The institution must use the format of the HMDA-LAR, but need not use the form itself.*		
5. An officer of the financial institution signs the HMDA-LAR transmittal sheet certifying the accuracy of the register's data. (Appendix A)		
6. The transmittal sheet is accurately completed. (Appendix A)		
7. The financial institution maintains its HMDA-LAR in its records for at least three years. (203.5(a))		
8. The financial institution makes its FFIEC-prepared disclosure statement:		
a. Available to the public at its home office no later		

HMDA Worksheet	Yes/No	Comments
than three business days after receiving it from the FFIEC. (203.5(b))		
b. Available within 10 business days in at least one branch office in each additional MSA or MD where the financial institution has offices, or posts the address for sending written requests in the lobby of each office in other MSAs or MDs where the institution has offices and delivers a copy of the disclosure statement within 15 calendar days of receiving a written request. (203.5(b))		
9. The financial institution makes its modified HMDA-LAR (loan application number, date application received, and date action taken excluded from the data) for the preceding calendar year available to the public, by March 31 for requests received on or before March 1, and within 30 days for requests received after March 1. (203.5(c))		
10. The financial institution maintains its modified HMDA-LAR for three years. (203.5(d))		
11. The financial institution maintains its disclosure statement for five years. (203.5(d))		
12. The financial institution makes available the modified HMDA-LAR and disclosure statement for inspection and copying during the hours the office is normally open to the public for business. If it imposes a fee for costs incurred in providing or reproducing the data, it is reasonable. (203.5(d))		
13. The financial institution posts a general notice about the availability of its disclosure statement in the lobby of its home office and in each branch office located in an MSA. (203.5(e))		
14. The financial institution provides, promptly upon request, the location of the institution's offices where the statement is available for inspection and copying, or includes the location in the lobby notice. (203.5(e))		
15. There were no errors in the previous reporting period. (Review the financial institution's last disclosure statement, HMDA-LAR, modified HMDA-LAR, and any applicable correspondence from the OCC, such as notices of noncompliance).		
16. To ensure that the financial institution has the necessary tools to compile the geographic information, it must attest to have done the following:		
a. If geocoding is performed in-house, the financial institution uses the U.S. Census Bureau's Census Tract Street Address Lookup Resources for 2000, the Census Bureau's 2000 Census Tract Outline Maps, LandView 5 equivalent materials available from the Census Bureau or from a private publisher, or an automated geocoding system in order to obtain the proper census tract numbers.		
b. If the financial institution relies on outside assistance to obtain the census tract numbers (for example, private "geocoding" services or real estate appraisals), it has adequate procedures to ensure that the census tract numbers are obtained when they are not provided by the outside source.		

HMDA Worksheet	Yes/No	Comments
For example, if the financial institution usually uses property appraisals to determine census tract numbers, it must have procedures to obtain this information if an appraisal is not received, such as when a loan application is denied before an appraisal is made.		
c. The financial institution has taken steps to ensure that any provider of outside services uses the appropriate 2000 Census Bureau data.		
d. The financial institution uses current MSA and MD definitions to determine the appropriate MSA and MD numbers and boundaries. MSA and MD definitions and numbers (and state and county codes) are available from the supervisory agency, the "FIPS PUB 8-6, Metropolitan Statistical Areas" (as updated periodically), or "A Guide to HMDA Reporting: Getting it Right!"		
17. If the institution is required to report data on small-business, small-farm, and community development lending under the CRA, it also collects accurate data on home purchase loans, home improvement loans, and refinancings in connection with property located outside MSAs or MDs in which the institution has a home or branch office, or outside any MSAs or MDs.		

HMDA Data Accuracy Worksheet

Use this worksheet when verifying the accuracy of HMDA-LAR data entries. To complete, review loan files and place a check in each applicable box. This worksheet can be used for reviewing audit work papers, evaluating bank policies, performing expanded procedures, and training, as appropriate.

When reviewing audit or evaluating bank policies, a "No" answer indicates a possible exception/deficiency and should be explained in the work papers. When verifying HMDA-LAR data integrity, a "No" answer indicates a possible violation and should be explained in the work papers. If a line item is not applicable within the area you are reviewing, indicate "NA."

Underline the applicable use: Audit   Bank Policies   Expanded Procedures

Compilation of Loan/Application Data					
Loan Name or Number					
	Yes/No	Yes/No	Yes/No	Yes/No	Yes/No
1. An identifying number (that does not include the applicant's name or SSN) for the loan or loan application. (203.4(a)(1))					
2. The date the application was received. (203.4(a)(1))					
3. The type of loan or application. (203.4(a)(2))					
4. The purpose of the loan or application. (203.4(a)(3))					
5. Whether the application is for a pre-approval and whether it resulted in a denial or an origination. (203.4(a)(4))					
6. The property type to which the loan or application relates. (203.4(a)(5))					
7. The owner-occupancy status of the property to which the loan or application relates. (203.4(a)(6))					
8. The loan amount or the amount requested on the application. (203.4(a)(7))					
9. The type of action taken. (203.4(a)(8))					
10. The date such action was taken. (203.4(a)(8))					
11. The location of the property to which the loan or application relates by (203.4(a)(9)): ▪ MSA or MD number (5 digits). ▪ State (2 digits). ▪ County (3 digits). ▪ Census tract number (6 digits).					

Note: *Collection of data concerning ethnicity, race, and sex is mandatory for all transactions unless the financial institution purchased the loans, or the borrower is not a natural person (a corporation or partnership). When an applicant does not provide ethnicity, race, and sex information in mail, phone, or Internet applications, the bank must indicate that the applicant did not provide the information. Data on annual income is mandatory for all transactions unless the financial institution purchased the loan, the borrower is not a natural person, the loan is for a multifamily dwelling, income was not relied upon in the credit decision, or the loan is to an employee*					
12. The ethnicity and race of the applicant or borrower. (203.4(a)(10))					
13. The ethnicity and race of the co-applicant or co-borrower. (203.4(a)(10))					
14. The sex of the applicant or borrower. (203.4(a)(10))					
15. The sex of the co-applicant or co-borrower. (203.4(a)(10))					
16. The gross annual income relied on in processing the applicant's request. (203.4(a)(10))					
17. The type of entity purchasing a loan that the financial institution originates or purchases and then sells within the same calendar year. (203.4(a)(11))					
18. For originated loans subject to Regulation Z, the difference between the loan's APR and the average prime offer rate for a comparable transaction as of the date the interest is set, if that difference equals or exceeds 1.5 percentage points for first lien loans and 3.5 percentage points for subordinate lien loans on a dwelling. (203.4(a)(12))					
19. Whether the loan is subject to HOEPA. (203.4(a)(13))					
20. The lien status of the loan or application. (203.4(a)(14))					
21. Reasons for denial. (203.4(c)(1)) If yes, the reasons are accurate.					

Laws

12 USC 2801et seq., Home Mortgage Disclosure Act of 1975

Regulations

12 CFR 203, Home Mortgage Disclosure Regulation
12 CFR 203, Supplement I, Staff Commentary
12 CFR 27, Fair Housing Home Loan Data System

OCC Issuances

OCC Advisory Letter 97-1,	"Home Mortgage Disclosure Act Reporting of Data"
OCC Advisory Letter 98-16,	"Accuracy of CRA Data in Large Banks"
OCC Bulletin 2000-35,	"Examiner Guidance" (Large Bank Community Reinvestment Act Examination Guidance)

OCC Handbooks

Community Bank Supervision
Community Reinvestment Act Examination Procedures
Large Bank Supervision
Sampling Methodologies
Truth in Lending

FFIEC Issuances

A Guide to HMDA Reporting: Getting It Right!

www.ingramcontent.com/pod-product-compliance
Lightning Source LLC
Chambersburg PA
CBHW080745290526
45790CB00008B/3327